To Dav—
I'm so thankful we found each other.

down to earth

LAID-BACK INTERIORS
FOR MODERN LIVING

lauren liess

photography by helen norman

Abrams, New York

contents

introduction

CREATING ALWAYS SEEMS TO TAKE ME BACK to childhood, when the days were long and anything seemed possible. As an only child until the age of fifteen, I spent a lot of time by myself outside, exploring the land around me. My dad built a tree house, and it was my pride and joy. I loved working on it, setting up pulley systems to transport things from one level to another, sweeping it out, forging new secret paths to it through the woods, and hanging out there with my friends. My mom helped me plant a "secret" garden in the woods, and I loved tending to it, getting covered in mud as I transplanted wild plants in and out of it. I was constantly picking the weeds and wildflowers that grew where we lived and arranging them around the house, or concocting home remedies and herbal teas with the plants I'd found. I remember how hard it was to pick the thistles, being too impatient to run back home for scissors and instead taking the pain of the prickly stems because the soft blooms were so massive and worth it. I was usually covered in mosquito bites and scratches, and I practically lived outside during the summer. I arrived home utterly exhausted and exhilarated daily.

Fast-forward to today, and I feel increasingly inundated with technology, various forms of media, clutter, and commitments, all of which seem to make life fly by and pull me away from the things that matter most. I find myself wanting to go back to a time when life felt simpler and slower, and each day was an adventure, where I felt more connected with what was *real*: concrete experiences spent appreciating the simple beauty this world has to offer, bonding with others, moments in nature, deep breaths and long exhales, taking in the land, experiencing new foods, being delighted by art and good music, dancing, cuddling, laughing till the hiccups arrive, and feeling something deeper than the everyday noise we're surrounded by.

Being outside brings me this little jolt of inner calm and strength that leaves me feeling ready to face the world with new ideas. It's a sort of mental exhale reminiscent of childhood days that gets me thinking and making plans yet fully experiencing the present moment. Over my life, I've found myself revisiting certain memories I've made outside, moments when it was still enough to simply take in the nature around me:

lying in the grass looking up through the tree branches, out of breath after running; eating chocolate chip cookies in the rain with my dad under the shelter of the tree house; taking in the "snow quiet" deep in the woods of northern Wisconsin; finding cloud shapes in the sky with my mom and now my kids; sitting in the cold sand and counting shooting stars at the beach with my husband; and watching my daughter see the fireflies lighting up a nighttime forest for the first time this past summer. These moments were completely ordinary yet entirely magical to me.

It's ironic that I design *in*teriors when my favorite place to be is actually *out*side, but I guess it's this passion for the earth that has so strongly shaped my interiors aesthetic. To me, nothing is more beautiful than what is naturally made: the sky, the earth, the seasons, the elements, and people. A home that celebrates its connection with nature and encourages those who live there to focus on one another and the world around them feels to me like it's fulfilling its true purpose; it's become the backdrop for a busy, beautiful, and very *real* life.

After years of designing, studying others' work, writing about design on my blog, and exploring my own personal style, I've honed in on what it is I value the most about "home" and living. My favorite kind of house feels relaxed and effortless; it's a home that is made to be enjoyed rather than impress, where humble materials and found objects are celebrated. It's a home whose style and soul endure throughout the years, where every last detail has been thought out so that nothing is wasted, where function and beauty are equally valued, and where there is an undeniable connection with nature and a bridging of the indoors and out. It's a home that lacks pretense and unapologetically is what it is. It's a home that is, in a nutshell, *down-to-earth*.

Down-to-earth homes have a simple, natural, relaxed vibe. They can be in the city, they can be

in the country, and they can be large or small. It doesn't matter what their architectural styles are, but they celebrate what's real and raw. I believe "home" should question everything: systems, daily routines, and each and every material selection and object coming through the door.

Home should enable us to slow down, unplug, have fun, let go, stretch creatively, and just "be," ignoring unimportant things like worrying about stains on the sofa or precious belongings being broken. It should welcome others without pretense. I believe in living a simpler, more relaxed life in which we appreciate the beauty around us and fully enjoy the present moments with those we love. Home should be there to comfort, to help, and to make life easier and simpler. *Down-to-earth* is not just a design philosophy but a philosophy of living.

Down to Earth explores the key elements of my aesthetic through a collection of homes in various styles that I believe embody the natural, relaxed, collected, and easy way of living I've come to love so much. I was fortunate to work with truly special clients and incredibly talented and dedicated teams of architects and builders on these projects, all with brilliant vision. I hope this exploration into what *down-to-earth* means to me inspires you to create your own carefree, easy, and, most important, *fully present* kind of life at home.

opposite An antique wine table is paired with my favorite vintage leather chairs over a painted cowhide in my design studio. I brought in massive asparagus branches and fennel blossoms from my garden and love using what I have right outside my door to bring life to a space.

ease

I'VE WORKED ON QUITE A FEW HOUSES over the years and have come to the conclusion that certain houses feel "easier" than others. Easier houses have a relaxed, stress-free, barefoot kind of vibe, where those in them feel completely comfortable kicking off their shoes and being themselves. These houses not only look good, but they're comfortable, being made up of relaxed, casual, and cozy elements, and they're typically owned by relaxed, gracious people. Those living in them have put great care and thought into the "setting up" of the home—the design, the decorating, and the organization—so that they can live more easily on a daily basis.

I've noticed that many of us feel relaxed and totally at ease when we're on vacation, in part because we're not working and we're focused on having a good time, but also because we're not dealing with all the possessions and routines that can bog us down at home. We've brought only our favorite and most useful clothing and personal items, our accommodations are typically stylish and uncluttered, and we have everything that we need and no more. Laid-back living, with a barefoot kind of vibe, where life isn't overrun with "stuff," is freeing, so why not aspire to live like this every day? How do we design a home so that living there feels easy and carefree? Setting up our environment so that it puts us in a state of physical and mental comfort requires careful planning and design and a conscious choice to be laid-back ourselves.

casual beauty

The kind of house I love invites all those who enter to exhale, no matter how casual or formal the architecture is. In an "easy" home, nothing feels too precious, which doesn't mean there *can't* be precious things, it's just that those things are arranged and displayed in a way that doesn't feel formal or stuffy, so that the mood is relaxed. To achieve this, I often juxtapose formal elements, like a gilded rococo mirror, with more casual, primitive ones, like a rustic wood console, for a bit of tension. Not only is the contrast unexpected and beautiful, but the casual element makes the entire composition feel effortless and relaxed. I prefer for major pieces of upholstery, like the sofa, to be casual and comfortable so everyone wants to hang out for a good long time.

Down-to-earth homes feel charming and loved but are far from "perfect." They're filled with humble and handmade things rather than fancy, perfectly kept pieces. Imperfections and signs of wear and tear are celebrated, and there's often a story behind things. Rooms feel as if they evolved over time rather than as if they were "bought" all at once. They're easy to live in even though great effort may have gone into their creation.

Down-to-earth means appreciating an old, worn kitchen table with years' worth of homework impressed upon its surface, soft, old jeans that fit perfectly, and walking barefoot in the grass. It's about recognizing that there is beauty and goodness in the simple and humble things. For so long, many of us grew up thinking that a "fancy" house meant it was a beautiful one; that columns, grand foyers, and crystal were where it was at. Not that those things can't be appreciated in the right time and place, but many of us lead casual lives, and they just don't "fit." Many of us move at a faster pace today, and we're often on the go. We're looking for an easier way of life that is still beautiful. We dress casually, and we speak casually—why would we not design our homes in the same vein? No matter how formal or informal the bones of a house are, through a series of choices and careful design, any home can be made down-to-earth.

worry-free

In the past, there was so much "precious" going on in homes, with "off-limits" rooms and unused spaces, whereas today, people are focusing on living their very best lives and truly enjoying their homes. We don't want to waste valuable time and energy maintaining and stressing about things in the home. As a parent in a busy household, I prefer for almost everything that gets touched regularly in the home to be worry-free, but I refuse to sacrifice style. I believe in incorporating quality goods that can handle what life throws at them, rather

than temporary things that will get ruined and need replacing—a sofa whose cushions will look and feel good for many years or a wool rug that can handle messy spills. I generally recommend high-quality upholstery that can take a beating in busy homes, because that's pretty much what my kids give to my sofas. I love down-wrapped cushions because they have a natural, relaxed, lived-in look and are incredibly comfortable.

Some of my favorite materials are linen, leather, and velvet. I often combine all three, because their textural variances make a room feel interesting to not only the eye, but also the hand. I love the casual, nubby texture of linen, which looks and feels natural and relaxed, and setting it against soft material like velvet creates an interesting juxtaposition that plays up the innate, contrasting qualities in both materials. Leather's smooth finish only gets better with age, as lines, scratches and other signs of wear appear. There are also so many new indoor-outdoor and stain-protected fabrics being introduced into the market each year that imitate linen, leather, and velvet, and the look and feel of these products keeps getting better and better, making them smart, worry-free options.

I employ slipcovered sofas and chairs frequently in busy households because the covers can be taken off and washed, which allows for the use of lighter colors—integral for an "airy" look—without fear of staining. A slipcover itself also has a slightly more casual feel, which helps impart a relaxed, down-to-earth vibe. My own slipcovered sofa at home is done in a white indoor-outdoor fabric that looks like linen but is basically bulletproof. I'm often asked how I have a white sofa with so many kids and dogs, and it's because nothing stains that fabric. When a muddy somebody—I'm not naming names—jumps up on the sofa, I can throw the slipcover right in the wash. I'm also very careful with material selections for pieces that see a lot

of daily use, like coffee tables and dining tables. I use wood finishes that are already distressed or very natural and will get better with wear and tear, along with hard-wearing materials like stone, metal, and glass. I often include natural-fiber rugs layered under wool rugs or cowhide rugs at home, because almost anything comes out of wool and cowhide, and the natural-fiber rug brings large areas of natural texture into a space. Having worry-free furnishings in almost every area of my home puts me at ease, so when accidents do happen I don't stress, because I know the house can handle it, even if it is home to kids or a messy fur baby or two.

Aesthetics, comfort, and function are of equal importance when making material selections in an easy, laid-back home. Elevating one over the others can result in an impractical, uncomfortable, or unattractive home, so the right balance of these elements must be struck. I learned years ago that I will always regret letting function trump aesthetics or vice versa. Some of my most practical choices have turned out to be my biggest design regrets, because how my house looks and feels is just as important to me as how it functions. Learning where your priorities lie by looking at your past decorating decisions can be an invaluable tool in anticipating future mistakes.

study of living

Organization is a key component of easy living. A home that's set up logically and thoughtfully, with things where they need to be so that they're accessible at the right times, makes living more effortless. Being prepared with both what is needed in the home and in planning out daily routines—in effect, being less "laid-back" and more "type A" in your planning—allows you to thrive and actually be more relaxed in daily life, rather than feeling like you're scrambling around looking for things.

I find it helps to study exactly how a day at the house goes for each person living in it, from waking up in the morning to going to sleep at night. Think of all of the decorative and functional details that can aid daily routine. Make sure there is a place for everything and go room by room, writing a list of any items that are needed to help the house function properly.

A reality check is often necessary to design for actual living, however. There's the way we *want* to live and the way we *actually* live, so designing around reality is key. Setting up a home so that it works for those who live in it requires an honest look at daily habits and routines. Waking up in the morning, how much time is there to make the bed? If there isn't much, it's best to be real and acknowledge that although you might want a perfectly layered bed filled with beautiful throw pillows, it's not practical right now. It makes sense to choose simple bedding that looks beautiful when made less than perfectly, with a well-chosen pillow or two. I set a small dish or tray on my nightstand to corral hair elastics and the LEGO pieces I seem to find around my room at the end of every day. In the kitchen, we keep dishes in the drawers so our kids can put the clean dishes away and set the table themselves before dinner, which makes life so much easier for me and my husband. I hang pots and pans and keep cutting boards out because I like things as accessible as possible. I noticed early on in designing my own house that our kids liked to play where we were, and so rather than fighting the fact that toys were being dragged into the living room, I added storage solutions—tables with baskets to hide toys in and an old dough bowl for the kids' books—in the living room to accommodate what was happening in real daily life. I realized the same thing was happening in the master bedroom, and so I keep a basket in there for quick toy-corralling at night. Do I like to think of the bedroom as a playroom? Definitely not. But in all honesty, is it used like one? Absolutely. I'm much happier now that I have somewhere to stash the toys than I was when I pretended toys didn't belong in my bedroom and they sat in a pile waiting by the door as if some sort of house elf was going to come and put them away for me.

Then think about weekend and entertaining routines and requirements. Make it easy, and keep entertaining essentials on hand: napkins, barware, and candles. Have a go-to routine for impromptu visits or dinner parties so there's no stress when they happen. My last-minute entertaining routine consists of "straightening up" (running around the first floor of the house with my kids picking up random toys and objects the baby or puppies have strewn about), fixing drinks with barware and mixers we keep readily accessible in a cabinet in the living room, putting together a quick charcuterie board (we keep a variety of cheeses, cured meats, nuts, and fruit on hand at pretty much all times), picking flowers or random greenery from the yard, lighting candles, and turning on music. Being prepared with all of the supplies needed to quickly get a party going and having a simple default plan makes prep easy and, honestly, enjoyable.

They're small details, but each one of these procedures increases my comfort and makes my daily life flow more easily so I can focus on the things that really matter: the people (and animals!) in my life and my work. At different phases of life, we have different needs, so solutions will need to be tweaked as time goes by and realities change.

joyful moments

Just as important as the functions and routines that allow us to live a more relaxed life is a laid-back atmosphere, made up of subtle nuances that cause you to let go and breathe easily. The way a room glows in the afternoon sunlight, a soft throw blanket waiting on the sofa, the pile of magazines you were leafing through right where you need it, the smell of fresh laundry, family photographs, a favorite painting, curtains blowing in the breeze from an open window, a crackling fire—all have an effect on your mood. All of these little scenarios, consciously or unconsciously observed, create moments of goodness or delight that put us at ease and bring us joy.

Thinking about what will bring about these feelings and transferring them into your design is what making a down-to-earth home is all about. Take the same organizational exercise of imagining life for each person in the home throughout the day, focus on each action from an enjoyment perspective, and think about how more good moments or little bits of happiness can be injected into the day.

We live in a drafty old house, and my husband doesn't like walking on a freezing-cold bathroom floor in the mornings, and so as we were planning our bathroom, we added in a heat mat under our tile before it was laid. It was relatively inexpensive, but it gives him a little bit more oomph in the mornings, and just that small bit of thought and planning went a long way in his enjoyment of our house. I could tell my little daughter loved yellow from the time she was a baby—that girl always picked the yellow stuff!—so I designed a yellow floral wallpaper just for her and had it hung in her bedroom. Now that she's a toddler, she lies in bed and talks to me about it, and when people first come to visit our house she says, "Come see my wallpaper!" I didn't realize how much enjoyment she'd get out of the wallpaper, but it truly makes her happy. In my kitchen, I generally like things as accessible and out in the open as possible, because I like the ease of just seeing something and grabbing it, so I've

made a conscious effort over the past ten or so years to only buy things I like enough to see out on a daily basis, including my pots and pans, bowls, plates, and cutting boards. Now, when I walk into a messy, in-use kitchen, I see a mix of things I love out and being used—a classic copper mixing bowl with tiny fingerprints on it, old wooden spoons, and a massive vintage cutting board littered with vegetables. Surrounded by beauty, I can focus on the people and the memories rather than on the mess.

learned calm

Part of "ease" is being able to put things in perspective. Not all of us are able to easily relax and just "be." Years ago, when my husband and I were newlyweds living in our first home and had finally gotten it livable and mostly decorated, I found I couldn't relax when things weren't where they belonged or a room wasn't completely "finished." As soon as I had a moment to rest, I spent it looking around judging what wasn't "perfect." I had to make a conscious effort to put things into perspective and force myself to look less critically at my home and enjoy simply being in the moment. It definitely helped and, for better or worse, I've developed a relaxed attitude toward perfection that has made life more fulfilling for me. Sometimes we have to coach ourselves to be okay about things, to be okay with the messes that come along with a home being truly used so that we can be at ease. Ease is a wonderfully contagious mind-set, and by being at ease, we can help make all who enter our homes feel it, too. +

left The shower in my good friend (and photographer of this book) Helen Norman's guesthouse, made from stone quarried on her and her husband's farm, is the epitome of laid-back luxe.

cozy bohemian

THIS HOUSE WAS DESIGNED FOR A BUSY family of five (plus a dog) who loves being outside. The wife is a free spirit who likes quirky vintage things and handmade objects. When thinking of her as I was working on the plans, I was continually drawn to oranges and warm colors. When we sat down for our first design presentation and she saw the various shades of earth tones and oranges I'd put together for the fabrics, she was shocked. Orange is her favorite color, and she said that she purposefully hadn't told me because she didn't want to dictate or limit the color scheme of the house, but the house ended up all orange anyway! Some things are just inevitable, I guess!

When designing an entire home, from the layout of the kitchen and bathrooms to the materials selections all the way down to the throw pillows, I find it helps to think of the house as a whole. I don't think, *Now it's time to pick the lighting*, or, *It's tile day*—rather, I think of the house in its "finished" state, which includes not only kitchens, bathrooms, and architectural details, but also furniture, fabrics, and objects. I need to see everything together to make decisions about even the very first building blocks of the

house. To me, design isn't a linear process, but rather, a large interconnected web that needs to get filled out. I think of it as a logical art, and when a change is made anywhere in the design, it affects the whole, so a potential ripple effect must always be considered.

In the case of this particular project, I knew I would be mixing colorful patterns in the textiles, so to keep it from feeling "busy," I selected neutral, mainly solid finishes for the hard goods of the house, such as tile, countertops, and flooring.

Throughout the project, we worked with a builder, Daniel Valencic, who shared our vision for creating something different and completely personal for our clients, to find lots of unique and reclaimed materials. Our clients' overall goal was for a strong indoor-outdoor connection and easy entertaining because they're such fun, laid-back people who love nature. **✦**

opposite The slight curve of the plaster fireplace creates a sculptural yet simple focal point in the living room.

IN THE FOYER (shown on the previous page), a bright vintage rug cheerfully greets guests. I had vintage pendants hung low to take up lots of visual space in the high-ceilinged room. A white oak sliding door opens to the library. A modern concrete console table and the intricately engraved silver Thai rain drum beneath it form an unexpected mix of the raw and modern with the embellished and storied. Paired with a bold vintage abstract piece, they create a casual, eclectic vibe.

Our clients knew they wanted simple, stress-free entertaining with easy access to the backyard and patio, so in the living room, shown here, the entire back wall can be opened up to the patio with accordion sliding doors. Slipcovers on the furniture can be taken off and laundered. I softened the heaviness of the doors with a pair of quadruple-width panel curtains in Gisele's Web, one of my favorite patterns from my textile collection. The larger the window, or door, the larger the curtain panel width needs to be so that it looks as if it can be pulled closed over the entire window.

AN UNEXPECTED combination of elements in spaces creates interest, so in the living room, which has strong and bordering-on-masculine bones, we introduced some more feminine and bohemian elements: whimsical botanical curtains in a clean, rustic space, and the gently curving plaster fireplace juxtaposed against straight lines and rustic beams. It's about shapes and patterns and creating a push and pull, or a yin and yang, between opposites. Simple inside-mount roller shades on the smaller windows keep the focus on the fireplace.

WHEN DEVELOPING the palette for our clients' home, I was drawn mainly to black, white, and warm wood and decided to have the wall behind the range tiled in black subway tile with black grout for a strong, bold feel. Faux-leather counter stools at the island—where the kids often sit—are easily wiped clean. This palette is carried throughout the entire house and makes it feel cohesive, carrying the desired vibe from room to room. I always design the kitchen first when possible, letting it set the tone for the entire home.

I love what I call a "glowy brown," be it in a wood tone, a leather, a textile, or a woven grass, because it adds depth to a room. I'm often after that perfect glowy wood or leather that really makes a color palette "sing." This can be seen in the leather on the vintage chairs at the kitchen counter top and table, along with the wood of the table and the rattan light fixtures on the next pages. They all have that glowy brown I'm obsessed with, and together, they create a warm, relaxing, earthy vibe. Patterned curtains and vintage rugs warm up the kitchen, add a bit of playful personality, and connect it to the open floorplan living room. Hanging basket lights above the table feel primitive and natural.

IN THE KITCHEN and family room, we incorporated reclaimed beams from an old barn to add patina and warmth to the brand-new space. I love beams as an architectural element because they instantly add a sense of age, character, and permanence to a home. I designed a "secret stool" niche on the side of this island so that the family of five could all sit there together. I'll often do this when additional seating is needed or when the cook in the family wants a spot to sit and work when needed. I used colorful rugs wherever possible in this house to add personality and patina.

A MASSIVE SOAPSTONE sink is a workhorse for washing loads of dishes—or hiding them when the realities of life hit! In the kitchen I had a pair of dishwashers flanking the sink paneled to match the cabinetry. I generally specify paneled dishwashers to ensure that the appliances don't "take over" the kitchen and blend in when they are in a prominent location. If they're in a less-prominent location I typically use stainless steel.

A COLORFUL COLLECTION of vintage paintings hangs in the dining room. Slipcovered settees on rollers pulled up to the table feel casual yet encourage long, lingering meals and make the dining experience feel cozy and intimate (and also provide a good napping spot for their pup!). When going for a light and airy feel—which I often am and was in the case of this project—I generally lightly sprinkle the wood pieces throughout a space. Just a small touch here and there in a primarily white room can help ground the space. In this case, the dining table, the natural woven shades, and the sisal rug.

A WOOD TREATMENT in the hallway creates a relaxed rustic vibe and is also practical in a house with lots of kids because it avoids the dreaded "hallway fingerprints."

A wall-mounted double utility sink in the mudroom is a striking focal point seen when entering the house, but it's the practicality of it that our clients love most.

In the library seen on the following pages, a pair of massive "wing" drawings above the desk spans over seven feet and creates a graphic focal point in a primarily dark room. The wood desktop—the perfect "glowy brown"—warms up the space and keeps it from feeling too stark.

THIS HOUSE IS generally light and airy throughout—with white walls, mid-toned white oak floors, and lots of natural materials and textures—but I like to inject "cozy" or moodier rooms in even the sunniest of homes to create a bit of a retreat away from the rest of the house, contrasting with the lightness, making the room feel more private. To set the library apart and make it feel warm and dramatic, we went with black walls, ceiling, and woodwork. Four cool-yet-comfortable chairs with strappy leather arms create a conversation area in the center of the room, and a desk lines the front wall.

As seen on the following pages, whitewashed old barn wood was applied in the hallways and stairways to add character and texture to what might have been an uninteresting area of the home and to relate the hallways.

Placing a sconce above art can make even the simplest of art feel special. In a hall leading to the kids' rooms, animal prints are set off by an inexpensive sconce above.

IN THE MASTER bedroom, a casually made bed with two simple throw pillows keeps the morning routine simple and streamlined. I often employ vintage ceramic bedside lamps that have an earthy feel to add depth and patina to a newer-feeling space.

In the master bathroom, shown on the following page, patterned encaustic cement tiles on the floor and an earthy glazed terra-cotta shower tile bring in both texture and energy.

Even the simplest, handmade objects can be elevated by their method of display, such as framing or by setting them on a pedestal. The kuba cloths on the following pages were framed in simple shadow boxes, which show off their humble beauty.

cozy bohemian

PROJECT DETAILS

architect

THOMAS FRENCH

builder

DANIEL VALENCIC
of Great Jones Build

get the vibe

- black, white, wood + orange (2, 6, 7)
- playful mix of patterns (2, 5)
- colorful vintage or vintage-inspired rugs (3, 7)
- free-form patterned curtains (7)
- warm, orangey leathers (6, 7, 10)
- slipcovered furniture (5, 7, 8)
- gallery walls of vintage abstracts (8)
- reclaimed wood (2, 5, 7)
- woven rugs, light fixtures + baskets (4, 10)
- oversize light fixtures (4)
- quirky objects (1, 5, 8, 10)

resources

- White walls and trim throughout: Benjamin Moore Super White
- Living room curtain fabric: Lauren Liess Textiles Gisele's Web in Apricot
- Master bedroom curtain fabric by Gastón y Daniela
- Master bath encaustic cement floor tile by Ann Sacks
- Mudroom sink by Kohler
- Upholstery by Verellen
- Rugs, case goods, pillows, and most lighting throughout are vintage

3

4

5

6

7

8

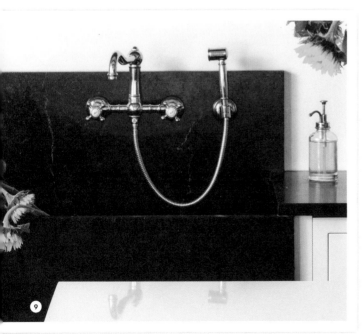

9

10

point of view

A HOME IS NOT ONLY A SHELTER OR A place of refuge, but it's an opportunity for self-expression. I've never had the type of talent I wanted at drawing or painting—yet have always loved creating—so when I found decorating, I realized that my home could be my canvas of sorts, and here was this chance to be able to "make something."

Why do we as humans create art? We create to communicate, to connect with one another, and to share what we believe to be true, in essence, to express a point of view. A home is like any other form of art and, like it or not, is saying something about those who live there. When you are putting the time and effort into designing a home, it is an opportunity to share a unique point of view.

That strong, clear point of view introduces others into a way of looking at the world. It's a sharing of interests, passions, histories, stories, and what is valued. It's fascinating to see and appreciate a perspective that differs from our own, one that calls attention to things we might not ordinarily have found value in, and forces us to recognize beauty and goodness where we

might not have normally looked. I like being introduced into others' "worlds," where it feels as if you're not looking at, touching, or experiencing the "norm," but rather are being let in on something uniquely someone else's.

project language

At the onset of every project, I begin with developing the aesthetic or key underlying principles that will guide everything we do. I come to the "project table" with my own aesthetic, my clients arrive with theirs, and the architecture, geographical location, and the history of the home all require attention as well. Interior design exists within a much larger whole, and it is most successful and powerful when the context of what surrounds it is taken into account.

I make a list of words or statements that describe all of the styles involved to create something that totally and uniquely describes my clients' project so that we have a "language" with which to work from throughout the project. It is kept at the forefront when making decisions, which helps to guide the entire process, serves as a

filter for everything going into the home, and allows me to discuss and describe how the home will look and feel with my clients. These words help focus the entire team of players in the project including the architect and builder. So many moves are made when creating a home that the better the desired final outcome can be verbalized, the greater chance there is of getting it exactly as intended. This applies to every type of project, from a single room makeover to an entire house renovation.

layers of interest

Incorporating interests and passions that represent a clear point of view into a home is not about impressing others; it's about self-expression. When we are creatively fulfilled by the home we have made, what results is a greater joy and a sense of pride and ownership. At times, thought, personality, or history are incorporated in an overt display—a landscape painting of a favorite beach or a family photo— and at others, they are nuanced, barely there, and only recognizable to those who live there—a mirror that once belonged to a grandparent or a fabric featuring a favorite flower. A home is made up of decisions, and just as much as each selection should be practical and make sense, these layers of interest should also help tell a story about those who live in the house and welcome them home from the rest of the world.

defy convention

A strong point of view is memorable and much more interesting than "perfection" or things collected simply because they're "pretty." I have nothing against pretty, as long as it makes sense for the people who live in the home. To me, a home is truly a work of art when it is truthful and honest, when it feels as if it's an extension of those who live in it, when it fits their lifestyle and shares bits about them, their motivations and their interests, and when it tells their story.

A strong point of view requires the confidence to make decisions that defy convention and are expressive. Expression of who we are within our homes isn't just about what we are displaying in the home; it's also about how we are using the home. Because we all grow up learning what is "normal" or "expected" in a home, it can be difficult to let go of that conditioning and live in the best way possible for ourselves. Getting a home "right" for *you* requires shaking off the shackles of "normal" and wrapping your head around how *you* live. For example, at my house, we use our dining room for eating, but we also use it for painting and kids' projects, so I now keep an easel and paintbrushes in there. Because I want the kids to feel inspired and excited about painting and proud about what they're doing, I've covered the walls in framed paintings they did. Having the dining room at the ready as an art studio means that we use the dining room much more than we did, because not only are we eating in it, but we're also

painting more because the art supplies are so conveniently located. For the longest time, the idea of storing art supplies in the dining room had never even crossed my mind, and in effect, I limited myself, because I was relying on typical "rules" for how to set up a home rather than on what made sense for me and my family.

Each time something is brought into the home, consider not only its functional purpose but also think about how it could be used to bring in personality and character. So many times, there is the typical "right" choice for something, which is generally in good taste and more universally appealing, and sometimes it's the way to go, but often, it's the choice that excites you, that reminds you of something, and that reveals something about you or your past that's "right" for you. Without risk and the confidence to make decisions that represent you, a home can't ever truly communicate who you are, and you won't ever truly be free to be yourself.

"Home" should make us feel like our true selves. It welcomes and protects and lets us be free to express ourselves honestly and meaningfully. How can it do this if it doesn't fit us and is communicating that we're someone we're not? What good does a shelf full of beautiful yet meaningless objects do? Or artwork that doesn't cause us to think or feel? A home that is an expression of who we truly are, no matter what "normal" is telling us to do, paves the way for us to be ourselves and to let go of all pretension. A down-to-earth home is about dropping pretense and living real life in the best way possible. ✦

opposite Old and new furnishings and fabrics mix and are pulled together with the thread of vibrant blue pulled from the framed guitar blueprint in Helen Norman's son's bedroom.

machine age maritime

OUR CLIENTS PURCHASED a dark, outdated, cedar-clad contemporary home on a local lake with plans to update and expand it. As we began the process of helping them figure out their aesthetic, we learned that he had grown up attending a turn-of-the-century Catholic school in New York City. He had come to really appreciate the beauty of the vintage Machine Age details of the school building and wanted to incorporate them into the home somehow. They also both loved that the house was on the water and wanted it to feel open, airy, and relaxing. Though the house is a contemporary home, we married these two styles into one very cool new thing. We collaborated with friend and architect Jim Rill to incorporate details throughout the home that embodied our clients' Machine-Age-maritime aesthetic.

The aesthetic was all about celebrating the beauty in functional objects and in the hard-working elements of the home. The goal was to incorporate both Machine Age and subtle maritime details without making the home feel like a stage set and making sure it fit within the greater context of its own architecture and the surrounding neighborhood, which is full of cedar-clad contemporary homes. Exposed steel posts and beams supporting the mezzanine with a punched-metal railing over the kitchen weave an industrial story throughout the house. The combination of hickory floors, soaring ceilings fitted with beams for warmth, and breathtaking lake views creates a unique composition that feels part factory, part walk in the woods.

The details that bring on the school-era memories for our client are there but not overt—the stair design inspired by one in a turn-of-the-century New York City building, the industrial brass tap in the kitchen, and the carved drainboard details of the soapstone countertop in the kitchen. The maritime details are just barely there, too—the paneling on the ceiling in the kitchen and the bedroom, reminiscent of a boat's hull, and the blue-and-gray color palette that pulls the water views in. Each of these little details that celebrates the function or mechanics behind the object itself or calls attention to the lake just outside the windows creates a meaningful and unique moment for our clients. +

opposite The dining area of the great room as seen from the mezzanine.

INSPIRED BY THOSE in a turn-of-the-century building in New York City, the stairs in our clients' lakeside home were made of rusted iron and wood. Their industrial vibe works with the contemporary architecture of the home.

In the foyer, an industrial steel dresser from the 1930s sets the tone for many of the Machine Age touches throughout the home to come. It's old and distressed, and even dented in spots, revealing bits of its storied past.

VINTAGE INDUSTRIAL and modern mix in the great room—from the new hand-blown glass chandelier to the vintage Tolix chairs in the dining area to the barstools reminiscent of old soda fountain stools. Nature runs throughout the home with its wide-open views of the lake and trees. We left the windows bare of curtains to keep the space feeling strong, clean, and industrial.

THE SHADES OF BLUE, ivory, brown, and gray in the great room were taken straight from the lake setting that surrounds the house. Whenever possible, I love to pull a house's color palette from the land right outside the door.

Vintage factory lights hang from the great room ceiling, seen on the following pages, where we added wood for warmth and character. Not every item in a home can be perfect or precious, but I try to make sure "statement pieces" fit seamlessly with the vibe I'm trying to create.

I TYPICALLY DESIGN the kitchen before any other space in the house, because I think of it as a microcosm for the entire home. Knowing that we wanted the house to feature classic, turn-of-the-century vintage elements, we combined soapstone countertops, vintage factory lights with prismatic glass, and four-by-four-inch subway tile that continues behind the glass upper cabinetry.

This hardworking kitchen was made for entertaining. A soapstone sink and surround with carved-out drainboard (seen also on the next page) is set into the massive butcher-block-topped island. Narrow wood shelving, seen on the following page, stores dry goods along with coffee and tea supplies, and wall hooks keep aprons at the ready.

White oak cabinet frames encase inky black-blue doors and drawers. I pulled in lots of black and deep navy in the house because the high contrast of the white and black/navy adds a bit of an edge and created a play of light and dark that is reminiscent of the light seen in old city industrial buildings.

down to earth

HARDWARE PLAYED a key role in this project, and each and every selection was used to express our clients' point of view. The industrial-style brass faucet feels utilitarian and strong. The black range hood is simple yet bold. A mix of metals, including brass, bronze, and stainless steel creates a collected, authentic vibe.

KEEPING THE FURNISHINGS in the master suite (seen on this and the next pages) clean and spare puts the focus on the powerful simplicity of the architecture and the views of the lake. Elements such as the accordion-style bedside lamps with exposed cloth cords add to the machine-age vibe. Light and airy unlined sheer curtains soften the bedroom, making it more romantic-feeling than the house's public spaces, and provide privacy when needed. A vintage leather butterfly chair mixes effortlessly with primitive pieces.

An antique sewing table (seen on page 81), another turn-of-the-century nod, is used as a console in the hall leading to the master bathroom and closet. I love giving pieces of furniture a use different from the one they were intended for.

down to earth

A PAIR OF HIS-AND-HERS vanities helps with the morning routine in the master bathroom. Custom marble "shelf" backsplashes are reminiscent of those in vintage bathrooms, while swing-arm task lights flanking the mirrors have

a turn-of-the-century library feel. Steel and glass shower doors call to mind large factory windows.

Larger-than-normal hexagonal tiles on the floor are a modern take on a turn-of-the-century classic.

Also seen on the next page, the master bathroom feels modern but includes nostalgic vintage elements, such as the tub, tile, and lighting. Simple planks of wood laid across the bathtub create a makeshift tabletop for a drink or a book.

open. Various brushes sprawled randomly nearby. Nail files and lipsticks protruded like pegs from the shallow top drawer, preventing it from shutting. And over all lay a film of fine dust, as if my client had sifted powdered sugar over the top. It resembled a haunted house more than a vanity.

You would think that people who own a vanity want it to look beautiful, yet in many cases my clients have turned them into a parking lot for their cosmetics. I don't own a lot of cosmetics and am a complete amateur when it comes to wearing makeup. Curious to see if there were any storage points that are specific to makeup, I had been contemplating going to the cosmetic section of a department store to interview the staff or asking a friend who was good at makeup when S came to seek my advice. This was perfect timing. S is a professional makeup artist. In addition to giving courses on the subject, she has also worked at the Paris Collection and as a makeup specialist for celebrities. She now has her own beauty salon where she provides personalized instruction.

The way she stores her cosmetics and tools is exactly what you would expect of a professional. When I visited her home, she had just given her vanity to a friend, and instead she had stored her makeup in a plain square box along with a folding mirror. Inside, the cosmetics were expertly divided into foundations, eyelashes, eye shadows and liners, lipsticks and glosses, and blushes. All the parts and tools were also divided by category. Whenever possible,

arranged so that every item was visible at a glance.

"I've divided everything into teams. Team 1 consists of the things I use daily, and Team 2 are the things I keep on hand to add variation. Team 1 has all the things I need to make my basic look complete, and I keep it in a pouch that I take with me for touchups whenever I need one," she told me. "If putting on your makeup is too much work, it's game over. The basic rule for storing makeup is to eliminate every unnecessary step."

She also kept Q-tips in a business-card case, and removed eye shadows from their cases to make her own original palette. "Dirty cosmetic containers are pretty gross. You should wipe any cases that contain powders frequently to keep them clean. If you don't, beauty will slip further and further away.

"As for shelf life, powders will keep two or three years once they've been opened. Get rid of lipsticks after about a year, when they start smelling oily. Things like liquid foundation, which are more like skincare products, only last about a year, too." From the perspective of a professional, the life of cosmetics was much shorter than I had expected. In my work, many of the ones I come across have easily been around for five years or more.

"There's no rule that says you have to put on makeup, right? That means if you want to wear makeup, you need to keep your motivation up. So it's worth getting some items that increase your motivation. The joy factor is

machine age modern

PROJECT DETAILS

architect

JIM RILL
of Rill Architects

builder

WOODHAVEN CONTRACTORS

get the vibe

+ warm industrial modern (3, 4, 9)
+ black + blue (5, 10)
+ schoolhouse furniture (1, 5, 10)
+ vintage industrial lighting (2, 8)
+ mix of woods including organic pieces, live edge + root forms (6, 7)
+ celebrate beauty in the functional (1, 7, 8, 10)
+ raw pipe plumbing (7)
+ a mix of metal finishes, including unlacquered brass, rusted iron, and steel (2, 3, 7)
+ layered rugs and patterns (4, 6)

resources

+ White walls and trim throughout: Benjamin Moore Simply White
+ Dining table and counter stools by Restoration Hardware
+ Master bedroom curtain fabric: Raoul Textiles Fulani in Ebony
+ Tile by Subway Ceramics
+ Upholstery throughout by Lauren Liess & Co. and Verellen
+ Rugs, case goods, pillows, and most lighting throughout are vintage

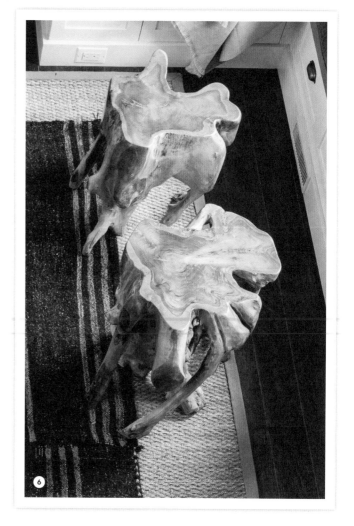

timeless-ness

I LOVE PORING OVER PHOTOS OF ROOMS done by the decorating "greats" of the past and seeing spaces that are just as amazing today as they were seventy years ago. Good art of any kind—be it a painting, a book, a song, a movie, or a house—endures and inspires long after the day it is created. It is timeless and true.

With the short shelf life of trends these days, in part due to massive amounts of exposure to new image after new image on social media, it's easy to tire of things. One moment everyone is loving something because it's "new," and then the next moment we're over it. Before society was consuming everything at such a voracious pace, things were appreciated for much longer. Today is like no time in history in that we have made so much that is meant to be disposable, and we have a constant thirst for what is "new." This can be an unsatisfying way of life: always chasing after something, only to finally get it and promptly get over it before moving on to the next trend.

As architectural and design trends and objects get taken out of context and overplayed, the innate "goodness" in what was being appreciated about them can and does get lost. Authenticity falls by the wayside as certain architectural styles and elements are taken to the extreme and installed in houses across the world, no matter their appropriateness. We get tired of the architectural style or element itself due to being overexposed to it, when really, we should be over the misapplication of it. I find many trends to be this way. There is *nothing* wrong with *any* authentic metal finish, be it polished brass, oil-rubbed bronze, iron, nickel, copper, or chrome; they can only be used in the wrong places, yet we will all be hearing about what metals are "in" or "out" until the end of our days. The same is true of architectural details, wallpaper, fabrics, stone countertops, wood, and pretty much anything else that can be brought into the home. It's possible to find unattractive and out-of-date examples of anything, but that doesn't mean that the category itself is bad. Every other year we hear declarations that wallpaper is "in" or "out," but the reality is that it's always "in" for those who truly love it, is always "out" for those who hate it, and it doesn't go in or out; it just gets overused in the wrong places, causing people to tire of it. The same is true of architectural details. Keep a house's origins in mind when making architectural changes, rather than focusing on what's currently popular, and the home can withstand the light-speed comings and goings of trends and remain authentic-feeling for its life span.

buy thoughtfully

Purchasing goods—whether old or new—is generally a part of designing and living in a home, and when it must be done, it should be done with intention. Everything we bring into the home can either make it better or detract from it. I try to think of nothing as neutral. Choose only furnishings and objects that will endure throughout the years. Think about things that would have looked good fifty years ago and that you believe will look good fifty years from now.

If you're unsure of what will endure, look at photos of interiors from your favorite books or magazines to educate your eye on what it is you're drawn to, and begin to ask yourself why you like it. Question if you will like the items you're looking at years from now. Study antiques and vintage furniture and notice the lines and shapes that you're attracted to. If those items are still appealing to you today, chances are they will endure and appeal to you years from now. Many antiques are timeless, and I find myself drawn to very simple, primitive ones, which can feel incredibly modern and fresh in the right interiors.

This applies to everything coming into the home, whether decorative or functional. As I mentioned in the chapter "Ease," there's the way we *want* to live and the way we *actually* live. In my house, the reality is that we see our laundry baskets quite a bit more than I'd like to admit. They often sit on the bedroom floor for a couple of days, waiting for us to put the clean clothes away, effectively becoming a part of our decor, as do a whole host of functional items that are

often bought rather thoughtlessly. For example, my broom and dustpan hang in my mudroom, I see my dish soap every day at the sink, and our food storage containers are used almost every night, covering my countertops before and after dinner, so no matter how carefully I "decorated," if I'm not selecting timeless, attractive, functional things for my house, the decorating I spent so much time and effort on will be eclipsed by the unattractive functional items I've brought into the house. Simple, timeless choices like woven baskets in lieu of plastic laundry baskets, a wooden pot scrubber instead of a bright plastic one, or an unobtrusive glass soap pump for clear dishwashing liquid at the kitchen sink help make the "real" view of home—the one most likely seen on a daily basis, where everything isn't perfectly put away and hidden—the best it can be. Being thoughtful and disciplined about purchasing timeless goods enables a more laid-back attitude about everything in the home, including "messes" being left out, because the house still looks good while it's undergoing the functions of daily life.

Vintage, antique, and used goods often add character and personality without taking a toll on the environment or the checkbook. Not everything needs to be precious, but the more we evaluate and expect out of what is purchased, the less we buy, the less time spent shopping for replacement items, and the less waste we'll produce. It's about purchasing carefully and responsibly, which begins with buying timelessly.

the need for change

Today, there are so many companies selling really inexpensive furnishings that it's easy to think of switching up decor all the time as "normal" or as the stylish thing to do. I definitely have a love for "change," and if I'm not moving houses—something I've done a lot of!—I try to focus on activities like arranging cut greens

or wildflowers from the yard or rearranging objects on surfaces randomly throughout our house, which helps me appreciate my existing things rather than purchasing new goods. I prefer getting the main furnishings and design scheme "right" in a house and then going on with living a full life in the home rather than obsessing over trends and changing styles to keep up with the latest and greatest.

I have gone through phases of constantly doing and undoing my home in the past—repainting rooms, changing up large pieces of furniture, and redecorating constantly—and it's actually what made me realize that I wanted to design for a living. If you find yourself doing this, and you realize it's because you truly love the process like I did, and your home is your only canvas for the creative urges you're feeling, then consider the possibility that maybe you were meant to do it for a living rather than continue to spend time and money changing your own home for the sake of change. However, if you think you're constantly changing things because you've made mistakes and aren't sure about how things are turning out, take the whole process more slowly and methodically so you don't have to backtrack.

patience

A home doesn't have to be "finished" to be lived in and loved. Have a plan for what needs to be done in the future, and be okay if you're not there yet. I'm years away from finishing my current home, but I'm trying to enjoy the journey. It's easy to purchase trendy items that fit in a room and fill in a need, but hunting for just the right pieces that will endure over the years takes time and patience. +

left Antiques mix seamlessly with wildflower-themed fabrics from my textile collection in Helen's master bedroom sitting room.

american soul

WHEN I WALKED THROUGH MY CLIENT'S door for the first time, I could see that the home was unique and that my client had an amazing eye. I loved all of the old oil paintings she had collected along with natural objects and timeless antiques. There is even a bridge on the property that she designed and had made out of branches she collected. The house itself was built in the late 1980s but feels like an authentic colonial home with slightly more comfortable proportions and floor plan. It was originally designed with integrity, having been inspired by a house the builder, John L. Hanson, saw in Chesapeake, Virginia, and is filled with authentic, period-appropriate details such as reclaimed heart-of-pine floors, antique beams, and the most beautiful old oil paintings hung on the walls. When we met, our client felt that the house was decorated too formally, wasn't comfortable enough, and didn't suit her, so we got to work modernizing the house and relaxing it to make it feel more inviting and comfortable while taking care to maintain the traditional vibe she loved so much.

We concentrated on painting and adding plaster and paper to various areas, changing out light fixtures, and decorating the house. We kept as much existing furniture as possible, bringing in new upholstery and more rustic pieces along with very spare sculptural ones to make the house feel more relaxed yet refined. Introducing natural elements and materials is a sure way to make a space feel more comfortable and casual, so we brought in natural-fiber rugs (jute and sisal) and raw oiled woods. We chose neutral, casual fabrics like linen and hemp and mixed them in with tone-on-tone natural-feeling patterns to lighten up the entire house.

Our very sweet client, whose taste is clean and simple, worried about introducing patterned fabrics into the house, but my team and I knew that once it was all in she would see that the subtle tone-on-tone patterns softened the house in just the way it needed. Little by little, as things started to come together, as painting happened and the first patterns arrived in the house, our client began to relax and trust. Now she loves every little inch of the house and says it feels completely "her." ✦

MY CLIENT HAS BEEN collecting beautiful antique oil paintings at auction for years and has an eye for selecting pieces with extraordinary depth and patina. We hung them in salon-style groupings and installed picture lights throughout the living room to showcase her finds. They're as beautiful today as they were a hundred years ago.

The old green-gold velvet on an antique chair only gets better and better with age. My client was pleasantly surprised when I said I didn't want the chair recovered.

The living room is a mix of my clients' existing furnishings and new pieces with clean pared-down lines. Soft, tonal fabrics in a neutral palette feel natural and relaxed.

BY MIXING IN comfortable upholstery and more relaxed pieces, like an old painted coffee table, with existing antiques, the living room is now the space where our client reads and hangs out with friends. We had the woodwork throughout the house painted in a soft greige color that gently contrasts with the chalky white walls. When going for a historical feel, I often have trim painted darker than the walls to play up woodwork. We brought in spare, sculptural elements like the small black floor lamps to help create an air of quiet simplicity.

An antique chest in the living room (seen on the next page) contrasts with the rustic coffee table in both color and style, creating a "collected" feel. Old sheet music sits at the ready on the piano.

WE KEPT all of the existing dining room furniture, reupholstered the chairs in a casual linen, and glazed them in a soft green-gray to lighten up and relax the room. New lighting, curtains, and rugs brought in warmth and our client's personality into the space. I love using the bits of gilt to add contrast and energy to cooler color palettes.

THE WELL-APPOINTED kitchen was mostly completed before I met my client, so all that was needed were a few finishing touches, such as the custom pot rack to house our client's extensive copper collection and the porcelain pulley lights above the old farm table. The mix of white, wood, and copper is timeless and in keeping with the rest of the home.

In the family room (seen on the following pages), branches cut from the forest liven up the coffee table made from an old wooden door. An incredible pair of Windsor chairs that were handmade by my client's brother add to the primitive colonial feel of the great room. They look delicate yet feel surprisingly sturdy.

The original fireplace was a deep red brick spanning wall to wall that made the room feel dark and cramped. Inspired by the kitchen at Mount Vernon, I had the brick stuccoed over to lighten up the entire room and at the same time make it feel both more historical yet modern.

A CLASSIC English chest in the foyer is layered with a handmade lamp I designed with my good friend Lindsey Augustine and chemistry glassware displaying cut leaves.

An antique spindle bed in a bedroom feels quiet and spare with an antique spindle bed and unframed vintage painted board.

WE PAPERED THE center hall of the Colonial in a large brown-on-brown paisley pattern by Schumacher to add earthy warmth.

In the powder room, we refinished the original pedestal sink, repainted—taking the greige "woodwork" color over the drywall under the baseboard to make it feel as if the lower portion of the walls are entirely paneled even though they aren't—and added a beautiful antique gilt mirror and a pair of graceful yet simple sconces.

american soul

PROJECT DETAILS

builder

JOHN L. HANSON

get the vibe

+ primitive Early American antiques mixed with English antiques
+ vintage rugs with natural-fiber rugs (5)
+ light, neutral upholstery and tone-on-tone patterns (2, 8)
+ spare, sculptural lighting (8)
+ reclaimed wood (1, 5, 10)
+ antique paintings in gilded frames (4, 7)
+ patina (4, 5, 6, 9)
+ muted colors (2)
+ woodwork painted slightly darker than the walls (3, 7)
+ old, earthy pottery, aged copper, topiaries (1, 6, 7, 9)
+ spare historical colonial (7, 10)

resources

+ Walls throughout in Benjamin Moore White Dove
+ Trim throughout in Benjamin Moore Natural Cream
+ Center hall wallpaper: Schumacher Madras Paisley in Tabac
+ Kitchen pendants by Circa Antiques
+ Table lamps in foyer and family room by Ware Clay for Lauren Liess
+ Family room pillows: Lauren Liess Textiles Fern Star in Sepia
+ Upholstery throughout by Verellen and Hickory Chair
+ Most rugs and case goods throughout are vintage or antique

7

8

9

10

some-thing old, some-thing new

SO MUCH IS SHINY AND NEW TODAY. "Shiny and new" can be okay, but it often comes along with the sentiment that if something isn't perfectly new, then there's something wrong with it. Life and time change things, for better or worse, so designing with materials and objects that have the ability to age well over time or those that have already begun that aging process promises that a house will continue to look its best no matter what life throws at it. Character in a home invites questioning and wondering . . . wondering about where something came from or whose it was before. Who made it? How old it is? What's its story? When it seems as if something has a history, it awakens an almost childlike curiosity within us.

beautiful tension

In an old house, life has left its mark on everything in the home—from the floors to the handrails to the hardware to the doors. It can be seen in cracked stone, verdigris copper, or a moss-covered roof—signs of age that only come about over time. I know whenever I come across a vine-covered anything, I instantly feel intrigued by the bit of mystery it has, sensing

that it's something that hasn't been touched in ages and feeling the urge to discover it for myself.

Patina also adds tonal depth on a visual level. When materials age, they often transition from a solid color to a variegated one. Think of how wood darkens on the edges as it ages, or how rust appears on black iron, or how white paper yellows over time; these variations in color create a new "blended color," as I like to call it, that has depth, as opposed to the flatter original color an object once was. Blended color can also be brought into a space through art (I often use "moody" paintings to achieve it), fabrics, plaster, and other materials. A room without depth of color will often feel "cold" and "new" and very "one-note," whereas a room that is filled with things that are made up of blended color often has depth and a "soulful" vibe.

For me, though, where there's a yin, I like a yang, and old, patinated objects and elements are most appreciated when juxtaposed with newer, fresh ones. Glass, mirrors, bright white lacquer, plain fresh-cut wood, and shiny, flawless metals like chrome can bring

COLEUS

about a truly interesting juxtaposition when mixed with aged materials such as old stone, rusted metal, cracked leather, or crusty gilt. I love an old, worn, wooden bed with nicks and scratches paired with fresh white sheets and bedding. I might like an antique quilt folded at the foot of the bed, but the bedding itself would need to feel new and fresh in order to keep the whole thing from feeling stale or stuck in time. On the other side of that same coin, I'd also love a sleek, upholstered brass bed paired with a faded, antique floral quilt. It's the tension, the juxtaposition, that's interesting and sets each element up in contrast so that it can be fully appreciated.

live for today

A mix of old and new elements also creates the sense that you are living for "today," for enjoyment of the present moment, rather than attempting to historically re-create someone else's way of life. Taking what is good and what is loved from the past and introducing what is appreciated today gives you the best of both worlds. Down-to-earth homes feel as if they were created effortlessly over time with the intended purpose of living rather than re-creating, and when everything is brought in from a single era—be it an old one or a current one—it will, by nature, be or become dated. Combining eras and styles to personalize furnishings, materials, and hardware results in a unique, more "real," collected, and timeless yet fresh-feeling home.

Mixing old and new is a bit of a dance, and there's no science to it, but I've found that I generally bring in new fabric on bedding or large upholstered pieces and vintage fabrics on smaller elements like pillows or chairs. I like old, patinated metal but also shiny, sleek metal and love to mix them together, especially in kitchens where the old and the new are often naturally joined, with the mix of modern

appliances and the homier elements of a kitchen. A down-to-earth home is about setting up your home exactly as you live in it, taking the best from the past and incorporating all the conveniences of modern-day living: a perfect marriage of the old and new.

the evolution of objects

Things don't have to be vintage or antique to develop a beautiful patina over time; they just have to be of a certain finish or quality. When buying new, think about selecting oiled or waxed woods and materials like stone or metals that get better over time as a full and busy life unleashes itself on them. Woods with more natural or "living" finishes tend to develop a patina over time and age better than those that are artificially finished, and when they do eventually change, embrace it. Learning to appreciate the patina of daily life on objects and seeing the beauty in imperfection is a part of being relaxed and enjoying a down-to-earth life at home. +

vintage revival

ORIGINALLY BUILT IN 1918, this historic American Foursquare was treasured by our clients long before we began the project. It's a special house, built with amazing woodwork and filled with beautiful arts and crafts details, but our clients wanted more openness and space for their expanding family. Like most turn-of-the-century homes, it didn't have a family room or a true master suite, so our clients began work with architect Shawn Buehler of Bennett Frank McCarthy Architects, Inc., to create a modern-feeling addition to their historical home that would incorporate a new kitchen open to a family room with a true master suite on the upper level.

Our clients have four little boys, so everything in the house needed to be toddler-proof while keeping with their aesthetic. They are drawn to midcentury furniture and prefer a modern vibe, but the traditional, turn-of-the-century bones of the house demanded attention, so we set about creating a house that would marry both arts and crafts and midcentury sentiments. My clients like deep, saturated color, so we introduced intensely saturated colors mixed with neutrals and warm, glowy browns into almost every room of the home. Using modern, family-friendly updates that kept an eye on preserving and celebrating what was already there, our clients are now living firmly in today with inspirational nods to yesteryear all around them. +

opposite The house's original oak mantle inspired many of the design choices we made throughout the project.

WE PRESERVED THE home's original woodwork throughout the house and added modern touches through the furnishings. The vintage rug in the entry hall is a prime example of "blended color," and it helps ground the space and give it depth. The warm patina of both the stair railing and vintage woven chairs brings character and interest. Green-and-white patterned curtains in an Erika M. Powell textiles pattern are fresh and playful. I absolutely loved the antique light fixture my clients had hanging in their foyer.

THE LIVING ROOM is papered in a scenic tree pattern that feels at once traditional yet modern and graphic. We recovered our clients' pair of Indian wedding stools in an intense green velvet, mixed in other shades of green on the sofa, and carried the green through to the palette in the back of the house. Modern, midcentury-inspired chairs are covered in a faded William Morris–inspired leaf-patterned fabric. The "glowy browns" (see page 30) of the mantel, cocktail table, pillow, and woven shades give the room warmth and depth.

down to earth

AS FOR THE KITCHEN, seen on this page and the previous pages, we wanted it to feel almost as if it could have been original to the house with just a tinge of midcentury-modern coming into play in the vintage soda fountain counter stools, glossy deep green island with walnut top, and stainless steel range hood.

Quartersawn white oak cabinets, inspired by the living room's original mantel, are paired with soapstone countertops and an extra-deep angled apron-front sink.

We furnished the dining area, seen on the previous pages, simply with an oiled oak table, modern Windsor chairs, and vintage-style cantilevered host chairs. Our clients found the vintage light fixture years ago. Painting the doors and windows black throughout the house helped unite the original part of the home with the newer, more modern part of the house.

OUR CLIENTS HAD FALLEN for a photo of an amazing contemporary room with massive glass windows and a wood-burning stove and firewood niches in front, and so the architect, Shawn Buehler, was able to re-create their "dream" family room for them. The sliding accordion doors seen on the left can be completely opened to the back deck for my favorite kind of indoor-outdoor living. Because my clients didn't want a TV in the family room all the time, a white TV screen is recessed into the doorjamb and can be pulled all the way across the doors to create a massive screen for a projector on movie nights.

A vintage red rug laid on the reverse to create a soft, timeworn look mixes with new leather sofas that will get better and better with age and an antique Chinese table. Handmade lamps by local potter Lindsey Augustine feel earthy yet modern.

The master suite hallway seen on the following page is wide enough for an old bench and a cozy red vintage runner.

THE MASTER BATHROOM, seen on the previous pages, combines black penny round tile, retro two-by-six-inch white subway tile with pencil-thin grout lines with a classic black claw-foot tub and lots of brass in the shower, where everything can get wet.

A vintage-style brass-and-marble washstand keeps the bathroom feeling open and airy, and all of our clients' supplies are in a closet across from the vanity outfitted for storage.

The master bedroom, shown here, is a part of the addition, and I love the quirkiness of its angles. The traditional black spool bed mixes with more modern pieces like the graphic navy kilim, woven leather chair, and angular task lamp for a true mix of old and new.

down to earth

WE FRAMED AND HUNG our client's collection of vintage Indian art, which includes airline menus saved by her mother from a series of Air India flights taken in the '70s and '80s, when the family went to visit my client's father's side of the family in India throughout the years. It's a graphic and colorful yet completely personal and sentimental focal point for the room. A down-to-earth home is filled with meaningful things.

vintage revival

PROJECT DETAILS

architects

SHAWN BUEHLER
of Bennett Frank McCarthy Architects, Inc.

builder

IMPACT REMODELING
AND CONSTRUCTION

get the vibe

+ black, white + a hit of saturated color (3, 6, 8)
+ Persian rugs laid on the reverse + kilims (6, 8)
+ wood cabinetry + a colored island (4)
+ painted black windows (1, 2, 4, 5, 7)
+ leather furniture (6, 7)
+ turned legs + bobbin furniture
+ schoolhouse-type lighting (1, 2, 9)
+ black + white vintage textiles for pillows (6)
+ vintage tables (8)
+ woven shades + curtains
+ personal art + objects (3)
+ being comfortable (5, 6, 7)
+ furniture that can take a beating (5, 6, 7)
+ perfection isn't as interesting as reality and quirk (3, 8)

resources

+ Walls throughout in Benjamin Moore Swiss Coffee
+ Trim throughout in Benjamin Moore Black
+ Living room wallpaper: Sanderson Woodland Toile in Ivory/Charcoal
+ Kitchen island in a custom-glazed color based on Benjamin Moore Rainforest Foliage
+ Kitchen lighting by Rejuvenation
+ Family room lighting by Visual Comfort
+ Upholstery throughout by Lauren Liess & Co. and Verellen
+ Master bedroom curtains by Jeffrey Alan Marks for Kravet
+ Master bed by Noir
+ Master bedroom leather chair by BOBO Intriguing Objects
+ Tile by the Tile Shop

down to earth

nature

"Everything made by man's hands has a form, which must be either beautiful or ugly; beautiful if it is in accord with Nature, and helps her; ugly if it is discordant with Nature, and thwarts her; it cannot be indifferent..."

—WILLIAM MORRIS

THROUGHOUT THE YEARS, I'VE FOUND myself going back to quiet, contented moments I've spent in nature, moments when I felt such a connection to the world around me and a thankfulness to be there, fully living and feeling. I strive to capture as much of that quiet powerfulness in my interiors as possible by harkening back to nature every chance I get. Nature is the most essential part of a down-to-earth home and my aesthetic. Nature's innate beauty is grounding and brings focus to what really matters, calming the soul.

In the constant battle between the "things" and noise of our manmade world and the rawness and quiet of the natural one, I design with nature at the forefront, which entails creating spaces that are quiet enough to let the nature around us speak up yet lively enough to captivate, bridging the transition between inside and out, and bringing natural elements into the home.

the indoor-outdoor connection

There is something easy and freeing about a seamless transition between the indoors and the out. Architecture plays a major role in how connected a home feels to the land it sits upon, with key elements like siting, windows, walkways, and material selections affecting it, but unless we're building from scratch or renovating, most of us don't have the ability to create or change architecture at will and have to look toward decorative selections to do the heavy lifting in connecting a home with nature.

Making the views outside paramount is one of the simplest ways to create the feeling of a strong indoor-outdoor connection. This can be done by orienting furniture toward windows so that the windows become a room's focal point. If you keep windows bare, the focus can lie solely on the view, whereas if you add curtains, you can soften and call more attention to the windows, making them appear larger. Flanking windows and doors with pairs of chairs and/or art or sconces can make them into an even stronger focal point, because the symmetry draws the eye to the center of the arrangement.

Let the composition outside the windows inspire the interiors. When the vibe of the home itself is in keeping with the nature it is surrounded by, the design feels more powerful

and true. When the colors outside, for example, are brought inside, there is a blending of in and out that makes the transition between the indoors and the outdoors feel more seamless, more natural.

If there isn't a nice window or view to take advantage of, "make" your own by bringing in a piece of art or a mirror. I like to incorporate as much as I can that's representative of nature, and I love both art made from nature and art whose subject is nature, such as old landscapes or seascapes, nature photography, and sculpture featuring animals or natural objects. I also use botanical-based textile designs throughout my projects, and my own fabric line is based upon my favorite "weeds" and wildflowers because, to me, even depictions of nature are inspiring and bring a bit of the outdoors in.

raw materials

I've always been drawn to furniture and objects that are evocative of nature. Whether they are new or old, I love things that feel as if they were literally plucked from the outside and brought right in—rough-hewn wood, raw stone, anything made from woven grasses, furniture made out of roots and stumps, and all kinds of natural objects.

The warmth of natural wood tones and woven materials is essential in creating a home that feels natural and relaxed, because it adds depth and introduces actual natural elements. Wood can come into play in many forms—in the home's materials selections, such as flooring, woodwork, or cabinetry, or in the decorative pieces, such as furniture or accessories. When wood feels closer to its natural state—for example, if it has a natural, raw-feeling, or aged finish—it feels more casual, relaxed, rustic, and organic. Think of the formality that a shiny, dark-stained wood dresser brings to a space versus the casual-cool vibe that a natural-oiled oak piece imparts. Neither is right or wrong, and both have their place, but when trying to achieve a laid-back, relaxed, natural vibe, wood in a more natural-feeling state that celebrates the wood itself is key.

I can't get enough of natural objects and am always on the hunt for them. My favorites include geodes, alabaster, pieces of wood and bark, vintage beakers filled with greenery, pressed botanical specimens, nature studies of any kind, nuts, seed pods, seashells, pressed leaves, preserved grasses, stones, coral, feathers, and living plants. I enjoy collecting natural curiosities as much as I love seeing them in my home. We have a flock of pet geese on our property, and in the summer, when they molt, we go for walks to collect the massive white feathers they've left all over. I display them in vases around the house like bouquets.

Material selections are important in setting the tone of a home. Woven fabrics like linens and hemp feel less refined than other fabrics and, thus, more natural. I adore neutral colors as much as I do the colorful ones, and this is because when a fabric is in a neutral color, it feels to me as if it's in a more natural, untouched state. It also allows for a play of textures where the focus is on how things are woven together and how they feel to the touch rather than on what color they are, and it allows the exterior views and colors to take center stage.

I frequently begin the base of a room with a natural-fiber rug (seagrass, jute, and sisal are my go-tos), because it's a natural material that instantly grounds the design and establishes a layer of earthiness in a room. I'll sometimes layer a statement rug over the top, which incorporates an extra layer of texture, depth, softness, and personality that can be communicated through the color, mood, or origin of the rug.

And finally, the simplest and often most powerful way to let nature in is to literally *let nature in*. Think about the four elements—earth, air, water, and fire—and how they can enter a home: windows and doors flung open in nice weather to let in the fresh air; a crackling fire or candlelit room; a hot bath, herbs, potted ferns, or cut greens and wildflowers set about. These natural elements have a powerful effect on our spirits, and they delight our senses and cause us to exhale. Take advantage of these simple yet powerful gifts. ✦

following Every wall in the back of the house is floor-to-ceiling and wall-to-wall steel windows, so that when you're inside the home, you almost feel like you're outside. The views, the colors, and even the weather affect the mood of the interiors on any given day.

quirky cool

THIS MODERN CEDAR SHINGLE–AND–GLASS structure is perched on a bluff on a remote island in the Chesapeake and was conceived with the idea of connecting the home with the surrounding natural landscape for our clients, a family with three children and a very sweet golden retriever, so they could escape the busyness of city life on weekends and holidays. Greg Ehrman of Hutker Architects designed the house to look like four original cedar-clad buildings that were connected by a glass-enclosed central living area. The view of the water can be seen from almost every room, and it is breathtaking.

Our clients want to be completely carefree when visiting, so all of the materials and furnishings needed to be able to stand up to water, sand, and vacation mayhem. My client loves color, and we looked to the surrounding landscape to inspire the fabric palette. She loves hunting for quirky, one-of-a-kind vintage pieces; she is laid-back, fun, and chic; and the fabrics, furnishings, and art needed to communicate her contagious joy for life. +

THE VIEW FROM the front door runs straight through the dining room to the water beyond. Simple forms allow the focus to be on the view.

The central area of the home, seen on the following pages, which consists of the foyer, powder room, dining room, and center hall connects the four main "structures" of the home. The sets of stairs lead up to private bedroom quarters—the ones on the left lead to the boys' bunk room and bath, and the ones on the right lead to the master suite. A third set of stairs is down a hallway and leads to their daughter's bedroom and a guest bedroom.

AN ALL-WHITE American flag hangs on the white oak walls of the structure that houses the powder room.

A floating concrete sink in the tiny powder room saves space and feels clean and simple. A terra-cotta tile wall protects the space from splashes and creates a bright and happy focal point that really expresses our client's sweet personality.

A PLAY OF TEXTURES exists in the dining room: ceruse oak inlaid with brass, raffia chairs, and concrete floors all combine (seen on the previous pages).

The cedar shingles from the exterior of the house seamlessly continue inside, bridging the indoors with the out. Black window frames help draw the eye to the views of the water outside. Textural raffia chairs and a vintage chandelier in the dining room add warmth and depth to the sparsely furnished space. The house is ready at all times for fun and entertaining.

A SCULPTURAL YET simple plaster fireplace is quiet enough to let the views and fabrics take center stage. The great room, also seen on the following pages, is broken up into several seating areas with a variety of seating types for either conversation or relaxing. The massive steel windows give the great room a conservatory-like feel, with the views being the main focal point. Large woven lanterns contribute to the playful yet natural vibe of the house.

Collected objects, both new and old, add warmth and personality.

LAYERS OF BLUE and green pull nature's palette inside. Patterns from my textile collection in shades of blue and white mix with Peter Dunham's iconic Fig Leaf on a pair of Lucite chairs, a shibori stripe on the back sofa, and a large blue botanical print on the curtains by Schumacher to create a playful boho vibe.

NATURE POURS into the clean, modern kitchen from multiple sides. I used a palette of white and greige and warmed it up with bits of brass, white oak, and rattan.

The island is concrete which feels clean and modern yet is textural and adds depth to the very "clean"-feeling space. Shallow shelving is set into the waterproof plaster surrounding the range. My client loved the prettiness of the Lacanche range, and I love how unexpected it feels in such a streamlined space.

I felt that it was important to maintain a feeling of seamlessness in the kitchen, so the backsplash was done in a washable plaster, seen up-close on the following page, that felt just like an extension of the walls, and the island was made entirely out of concrete. A deep shelf below, seen on the next page, stores dishes in plain sight, so guests can easily help themselves and feel welcome in the kitchen.

The dining room, seen on page 177, is spare and simple to let the nature outside shine.

ICHTER

ORESATANNA HAUTE BOHEMIANS

HIST
M

HISTORY OF MODERN ART
JANSON
SECOND EDITION
PRENTICE-HALL · ABRAMS

THE COLOR FIELD PAINTINGS

NG COUNTRY, CITY, COAST
KNOPF

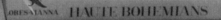
ABOVE THE WORLD

BURL WOOD is a favorite material of mine because of its depth and warm "glowiness." It sets off the books and humble objects on the coffee table, elevating them to "art."

The family room is a bit removed from the central area of the house, and we added shades of blush and orange to warm it up and make it feel cozier for curling up and watching movies.

The vanity wall of the master bathroom, as seen on the following pages, backs to the headboard of the bed and is fitted into a wall of steel windows, allowing the sunlight and views from the master to pour into the bathroom.

AN OLD OAK TREE on the property frames the water views from the master bedroom. I pulled green into the fabrics to create as seamless a transition as possible between the outside views and the bedroom itself. The bedroom feels as if it's a tree house.

A penshell headboard, seen up-close on the following page, adds earthy character to the mostly white, open space. Pivoting wall lamps save space on the narrow nightstands. I used a traditional floral linen by Clarence House on a midcentury Italian chair to create an unexpected traditional twist on a very modern chair.

THE MASTER BEDROOM is all about the views. Sheer linen curtains soften the steel of the massive windows.

The master bathroom is quiet and serene except for the prettily patterned shower walls, which add a bit of fun energy to the space.

Pastels reign supreme in our clients' daughter's bedroom suite, seen on the following pages. The rattan bed adds a bit of earthiness to help ground the sweet, bubblegum color palette. In her bathroom, a white oak vanity mixes with hand-painted terra-cotta tile flooring and simple white subway tiles. We kept the vanities throughout the house very similar, to keep it feeling cohesive, and brought personality in through tiles, mirrors, and lighting. The playful patterned floor and mirror work with the cheerful, colorful vibe of her bedroom.

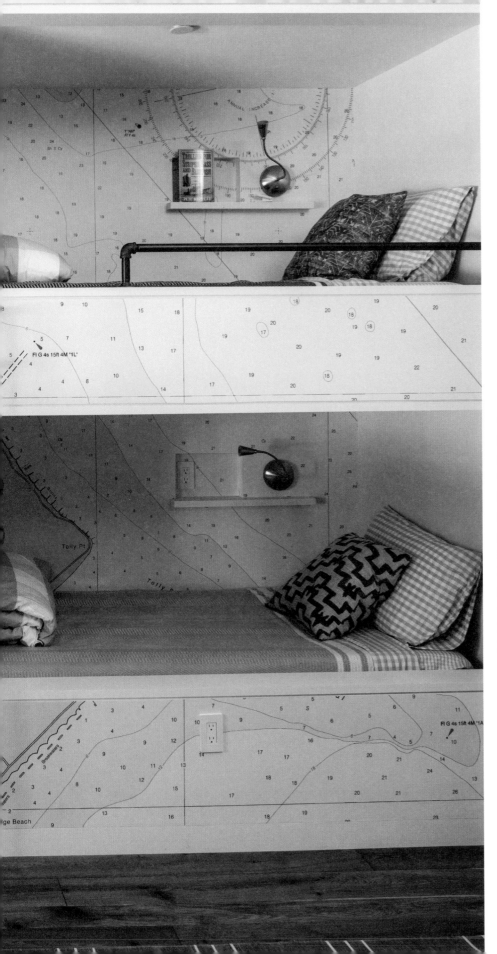

THE BUNK ROOM, seen here and on the following pages, is papered in custom nautical chart wallpaper by "Skipper" Steve Morris. It features local waterways and has eight sleeping nooks for the kids and their guests. Extra-wide single ladders made from pipe lead to the upper bunks. The kids wanted an all-out nautical-feeling space, so we filled it with authentic maritime elements like vintage life preservers and lanterns with cage guards.

A CLEAN AND SIMPLE guest bathroom with an airy black, white, and wood palette, that is in keeping with the adjoining bedroom, which is spare and understated, complete with a hanging leather headboard by Casamidy and a calming palette of black, ivory, brown, and blush.

quirky cool

PROJECT DETAILS

architect

GREG ERHMAN
of Hutker Architects

builder

THE BANKS DEVELOPMENT CO.

get the vibe

+ white, natural woven materials + bright colors (8)
+ lively mix of patterns with a white background (7, 8, 10)
+ boldly patterned upholstery (10)
+ chinoiserie elements (8)
+ big, bold art (3)
+ midcentury case goods (5)
+ woven furniture, rugs, baskets, lights (5, 8, 9)
+ the use of concrete (4)
+ textural whites (2, 8)

resources

+ Walls throughout in Benjamin Moore Super White
+ Master bath tile by Ann Sacks
+ Upholstery by Verellen
+ Great room pendants by Palecek
+ Great room curtains: Schumacher Palampore Block Print in Sapphire
+ Great room patterned chairs by Vanguard in Peter Dunham Textiles Fig Leaf
+ Great room settee by Serena and Lily with velvet by GP&J Baker in Barcelona in teal
+ Great room pillows in Lauren Liess Textiles and vintage fabrics
+ Kitchen lighting by BOBO Intriguing Objects

+ Master bedroom quilt in Les Indiennes
+ Master bedroom chair by Castelli is vintage and upholstered in Clarence House Dahlia Hand Block in Green
+ Custom bunk room chart wallpaper by "Skipper" Steve Morris
+ Bunk room lanterns by Visual Comfort
+ Patterned floor tile in bathrooms and on powder room wall by Tabarka
+ Vintage rugs, case goods, and fabrics included throughout

down to earth

sim-
plicity

WITH THE HECTIC PACE OF LIFE TODAY, I feel the constant urge to simplify my life and home to make space—both physically and mentally—for what truly matters. When I started my blog all those years ago, I named it *Pure Style Home*, and my motto was "Simple, happy, beautiful." "Simplify your life" was printed on my first set of business cards, because, even then, I felt that a pure, simple style and way of living was the key to happiness at home. My grandfather on my dad's side—my "nonno," as we called him—was always telling the family to "keep it simple," and I still marvel at the beautiful simplicity and organization of both sets of my grandparents' lives. Frugal with themselves and generous with everyone else, they all have only what is needed and take great care with their homes, gardens, and possessions, with their purchases, and with their wonderfully yet simply prepared meals and flower arrangements. My two grandmothers are my design inspirations because of the graceful yet simple way they choose to live in their homes.

As I've worked with clients throughout the years, I've found that many of them, too, are seeking to achieve a simpler life through the design of their houses. Simplicity lies at the core of living a more relaxed life at home. Simplicity of design (in composition, restraint, and strong editing) and physical simplicity (a lack of clutter, living with less, and having only what is needed or loved) are *both* key in making the most of each day and living the best possible life at home.

the power of restraint

My favorite rooms are marked by a powerful simplicity, one that is quiet but strong enough to hold its own and captivate. I like empty space to contrast with areas or elements of interest. I appreciate simplicity in the purity of materials and details, raw edges, natural finishes, and displays that celebrate the essence of things.

Simple spaces generally have an air of "breathing room," no matter how large or small they are. It's not always that they have a lot of physical space, but that there is enough empty space for the eye and the mind to rest. Larger but fewer pieces can help a small room achieve a feeling of airiness. For example, in a smaller room, a larger sofa going almost wall to wall—as opposed to a small sofa with tiny end tables and space on the sides—looks clean and makes the room feel more spacious. One large item stretched over a space actually makes the space appear wider, because horizontal lines—such as those of a long, low sofa—have this effect on a space, whereas just the opposite is true, and vertical lines—like those of vertical paneling—make an area feel taller and narrower. Opt for spacious walkways of three feet or more for a feeling of ease as you move throughout the room. Tripping over furniture or having to squeeze by something unconsciously makes us feel as if we have to be careful, which is the exact opposite of how we should feel in a down-to-earth home.

As beautiful as a surface styled to every last inch with interesting objects and flowers is, I find that I'm much happier in daily living when I've accessorized with a light hand, using restraint and making sure there is room to set things down and function. Simplicity allows space for life. It's about making sure each selection is doing its part and no more, no less. It's a balance. Some elements need to be heard loud and clear, while others need to whisper, and *all* are of equal importance to the whole.

physical simplicity: living with less

I wish I could call myself a minimalist, but I am someone who loves my "things." I've always loved chronicling life through writing and photos and in the collection of objects. I get sentimentally attached and associate memories with things like art, photos, books, sculpture, rugs, textiles, and even old perfume. I don't bring much new into my home, but over time, holding on to pieces from the past, I need to constantly edit to keep my memory hoarding from getting the best of me. I attempt to subscribe to a way of living where I constantly assess each and every thing coming

into our home. I am happier with less, when I don't feel as if I am beholden to my things. Still, I'm no minimalist.

It's not about placing a limit on the quantity of things that can be in the home; it's about creating a stipulation for everything that resides there. In 1834, designer, pattern maker, and philosopher William Morris wrote, "Have nothing in your houses that you do not know to be useful or believe to be beautiful," and when purging, as a practice, I try to ask myself if what I'm holding is useful or beautiful, and I generally attempt to only keep things that are both. Over time, it's become easier and easier to part with things, and I've realized that buying doesn't excite me anymore, but getting rid of things does. My idea of a fun Saturday ten years ago used to be shopping, but now it's decluttering.

Simplicity in the sense of living with less and keeping only what we find value in makes life easier and more fulfilling. When there is less, however, more attention must be paid to what is going into a home, because there is more focus on what is there. Everyday things can feel a bit elevated when there aren't too many of them. My goal is to only have things that are long-lasting and trend-proof. I won't pretend that everything that comes through the door will have meaning, but I do like for as much as possible to have that sort of "modern heirloom" quality about it, where even the humblest of objects is worth keeping and using for years and years. It's not about buying expensive things though; it's about buying only what you need and love. The house and its contents shouldn't exist purely for function, but rather they should bring us joy and make daily life feel a little better. ✢

ancient modern

YEARS AGO, WHEN MY COUSIN FIRST ASKED me for help with his home in Florida and he showed me the architectural plans he'd had drawn up, I honestly couldn't have imagined a less down-to-earth home if I'd tried. No fault of the architect's, because it was just what the client (my cousin) had asked for, but it was *massive*. I mean really, excessively, uncomfortably large. I asked him to show me photos of houses he loved, and I was inundated with image after image of dark, opulent mansions filled with crystal, gold, and curled wrought-iron architectural details. Maroon and brown were everywhere, and all of the furniture was massive, dark, and heavy. Whenever I'd get a text of a room he loved, I'd brace myself. My cousin would have lived in a fourteenth-century castle swathed in burgundy velvet if he could have.

The problem with this—other than there was no way I'd help him create *that* in my spare time—was that this guy is barefoot and in shorts the majority of the time, spending most of his days outside working or on the water, constantly entertaining friends and family in a gracious, laid-back, casual way. As one of three children

of a single mom, my dad's sister, he started his lawn business when he was only eight years old and kept it going all throughout high school and college. Even though the business has now grown into a large commercial landscaping firm, he still works with many of his original clients and his first three employees. His idea of "dressing up" is putting on a pair of jeans and a long-sleeved T-shirt. He has a pet squirrel named Bernie who rides around on his shoulder. He wants to have kids and for them to grow up in this house. These seemingly Dracula-inspired mansions he was showing me made zero sense with who he really was. The house he was building was completely unaligned with his true lifestyle.

We've talked about it over the years, and I asked him recently why he originally thought he needed something like that. He said he just believed that these types of homes were a sign of security, that the people living in them had "made it." Having felt financial struggles throughout his childhood, he wanted to show that he'd succeeded and believed it was what he was *supposed to* have. I find a lot of people do what they think *should* be done or have visions of proving something, but once they realize

opposite The center hall is made architecturally interesting with a series of groin vaults and classic iron lanterns, so I kept it simple and spare so as to not draw attention away from the architecture.

none of that matters and can let it all go, they can live as who they really are.

I felt like it was my mission to get my cousin to a lighter, more authentic place where he could be free to be himself and drop the pretension he was after. My cousin is like a brother to me, and nothing is ever sugarcoated between us, so I let him know that there was no way I would help him unless he gave me the reins to the project. He would GC, but he had to trust and let me design the house as I wanted, and there was no way he'd be getting a dark red mansion from me. As harsh as this sounds, I felt I had to get him out of his own way and that he'd thank me for it later.

The majority of the architecture was already in place when I came aboard the project: the floor plan, the exterior, the ceiling heights and windows, but I came on just in time to select the finishes and materials we'd use throughout, such as the moldings (or lack of moldings), ceiling details such as groin vaults and barre vaults, doors, cabinetry, and hardware. I saw right away that my cousin was attracted to classical forms and beautiful old villas but had only been exposed to them in the form of modern faux-Dracula-Tuscan mansions, so if we could just pull out the timeless classicism he loved so much and combine it with the more clean-lined modern home he'd had drawn up by the architect, we could get to a place that made sense.

When I got down to the bottom of why he would build such a big house—other than the fact that he felt he was "supposed to"—it became obvious that entertaining was a major factor—impromptu get-togethers, family reunions, or even weddings for friends. The majority of the house's square footage is dedicated to entertaining areas—including a bar and wine room—and lots of guest bedrooms for family and friends who come to stay. He's never happier than when he's making others happy and showing them a good time.

opposite My cousin's pet swan, Pretty, swims in a pond on the property.

Because the bones of the house felt so brand-spanking-new, I didn't want to fight with that. There was no pretending this was an old house, and I felt that a fresh white palette was the most honest approach to the house. I believed that if I mixed in antiques and elements with patina and depth, like antique limestone floors from Jerusalem along with pecky cypress beams and cabinets, they would stand out and be appreciated against the white museum-like walls.

It was also important to me that the pieces we brought into this house had meaning. At the onset of the project, the house felt like a massive empty shell, and my cousin's first inclination was to fill it all up as soon as possible, which just didn't feel right to me. He's not someone who's attached to stuff, so when he moved in, he didn't bring much with him. The house echoed, and I'm sure it was pretty lonely. He'd text, *Cuz, when are you going to pick stuff out for my house?!* Slowly but surely, we collected things over the years. We'd visit antique stores together, and he'd video call me whenever he was shopping on travels so I could shop with him. Something about how large and massive this white box of a house was made me feel like the things coming in could almost fill it with *their* stories and their mysterious pasts, so it all needed to be meaningful and special.

It took us years to amass everything for the house, and I spent so many nights and weekends working on this "side project," but my cousin recently told me that no matter what kind of day he's had or what's been going on, when he comes home, everything feels instantly "okay." And to me, that's what home is; it's the place that helps us feel okay and right, and at peace. . . . Free to be exactly who we are with zero pretenses. And so I'm glad I got to go on this journey with my cousin and that he's finally got this place he can just be "him" in, squirrel and all. ✦

ONE OF MY FAVORITE memories in this house was when my cousin proceeded to "play" Journey's "Don't Stop Believin'" on the piano for my then-nine-year-old son who was blown away by his "talent" until he lifted up his fingers and the piano kept on playing. I'm pretty sure he bought it strictly for the purpose of pranking his friends and loved ones. In the foyer, shown on page 213, an antique Flemish tapestry adds depth and patina to the very "white" space. A chocolate suede bench is flanked by kumquat trees in massive old planters.

THE LARGE WALL in the great room, seen on this and the previous page, had the potential to overwhelm the eye, so to fill it in, yet keep it feeling light and airy, we collected antique plaster and carved stone pieces for years to hang over thirty feet high.

The view seen when walking in from the front door is through the great room, shown here, and straight out into the tropical beauty of the backyard and pond. The mantel is antique, and the pairs of chairs, coffee table, and rug are vintage. Hand-block-printed curtains in a fabric by Les Indiennes soften and warm the massive white space. I wanted it to feel as if the outdoors were beckoning you out in every room of the house.

THE BARREL-VAULTED dining room ceiling, seen here and on the previous pages, was one of my cousin's few nonnegotiables, and I was more than happy to oblige. Reclaimed stone from Israel adds natural texture and warmth, and a long table accommodates big, loud, Italian family meals.

Antique Italian oil paintings, a statue of John the Baptist, and mismatched antique Spanish chairs, also shown on the previous pages, were combined with a new dining table, chandelier, sideboard, and lamps. I added curtains all around the room to soften the harshness of the hard stone.

Simple and practical stoneware mix with a sprouting coconut on the bare table. My cousin rarely entertains formally but the dining room is an inviting spot for large, casual family meals.

REPETITION AND symmetry are some of simplicity's best tools. In the kitchen, the symmetrical shelves flanking the stone-clad chimney-style range hood draw the eye straight to the range. The repetition of the same light fixtures over both islands keeps the look simple and uncluttered. The islands and beams are made from pecky cypress, which is native to Florida. My cousin is an amazing cook, and my favorite spot to hang is on the sofa-like counter stools while he's whipping something up, most notably grilled avocados with freshly caught conch fritters.

THE BREAKFAST NOOK is decorated simply with warm, glowy brown leathers, wood, and strong vintage black-iron chairs. My cousin salvaged antique doors, and we hung them to look like interior shutters.

The house has the potential to feel "grand," but casual elements like the incredibly deep sofa, layered rugs, and woven coffee table in the family room, seen on the following pages, bring it back down to earth and make it feel more gracious and welcoming.

I LOVE FORAGING outside to style surfaces. A large stone bowl on the vintage rattan coffee table is filled with seed pods we found on the property.

Incorporating spare, simple pieces like this handmade iron wall console I had made and juxtaposing them with more ornate feminine pieces like the gilded mirror above it creates an appealing yin-yang effect.

MY COUSIN and I found a pair of old woven birdcages while out shopping and had them turned into hanging light fixtures for the fireplace niches. The piece over the fireplace was made by artist John Anthony Scerbo out of concrete to resemble cracked volcanic rock. Super comfortable white leather chairs are big enough for two.

THE WALL OF DOORS in the family room opens completely to the loggia, pond, and coconut grove just beyond, and it truly feels as if you're outside when you're inside.

In the party room, seen on the following page, the simple concrete bar is always stocked with not only drinks but, to the delight of visiting kids, ice cream!

The same stone used throughout the house lines the walls and ceiling of the wine room seen on the following page. We had square niches created in the walls and fitted rebar inside them to store wine bottles. A simple skirt under the concrete countertop hides less attractive boxes and supplies.

I LOVE TO MIX the soft with the strong to create interest and tension. In the bedroom seen on the previous pages, a spare wrought-iron bed is softened by a gauzy white bedspread and layers of hand-block-printed curtains, and a raffia dresser is paired with vintage gold lamps and understated black shades.

A feeling of seamlessness was important to me when designing the house, so to keep the architecture as clean-feeling as possible, there is a lack of trim details, including baseboards and door and window trim, throughout. In the master bathroom, shown here and on the following page, vanities are formed out of the same plaster as the walls for a continuous, seamless feel.

A vintage Moroccan lantern hangs from the center of a groin vault, and a reproduction of an antique Italian stone fountain has been turned into a bathtub in front of the windows with a secondary rain showerhead above it.

I wanted the showers to feel almost cave-like or as if they had been carved from stone, so the shelves and benches are coated in the same waterproof plaster, which has so much depth of color.

AN EMBOSSED GOLD bed in the guest bedroom shown on the previous spread is mixed with retro-feeling nightstands, a woven light fixture, earthy pottery lamps, and lots of white for a spare yet collected feel.

I made a bit of a departure in this guest bedroom seen left (where I stay when I visit!) by pulling in a collection of vintage tropical landscapes to add a little color and fun. My cousin has lots of visitors from colder climates and so I really wanted this room to give a nod to Old Florida.

Almost every element in this room consists of an interesting texture—the woven light, the Martha Washington bedspread, the raffia nightstands, the twig mirror. I wanted it all to feel tactile and touchable.

BERNIE, MY COUSIN'S pet squirrel (above) checks himself out in the mirror. Fresh roses from my aunt's garden roused his curiosity. He has a special "house" but also runs free some of the time.

The clean white bunk room, opposite, was designed for visiting nieces and nephews and is a favorite hangout spot for my kids, four of whom are shown here. I kept it intentionally spare and simple with the green palm curtains and pillows being the only color in the space so that their inevitable "travel mess" feels a bit more manageable.

ancient modern

PROJECT DETAILS

architect

JOHN LAMB

builder

ADAM BAKER

get the vibe

+ easy breezy (7, 8)
+ white drywall/plaster (6)
+ lack of trim/rounded drywall corners (5)
+ big, soft, washable slipcovered upholstery in white + beiges (7)
+ spare wrought-iron details in items: lighting, decorative objects, etc. (2, 4)
+ sculptures, old + new (3, 6)
+ plaster pieces (6)
+ layered rugs (8, 9)
+ repurposed antique or vintage pieces (1, 3, 4, 5, 7, 8, 9)
+ European antiques (3, 5, 6, 9)
+ Mexican woven pieces
+ Spanish leather chairs (5, 9)
+ cracked old brown leather (5, 9)
+ antique oil paintings
+ tapestries (1)
+ gold accents (2, 5)

resources

+ Walls throughout in Benjamin Moore Snow White
+ Great room curtain fabric by Les Indiennes
+ Family room curtains by Lauren Liess Textiles Mothwing in Moss
+ Upholstery by Verellen

+ Iron bed by Tara Shaw
+ Gold bed by Anthropologie
+ Floors and reclaimed stone by Ancient Surfaces
+ Antique fireplace from Laurier Blanc

down to earth

6

7

8

9

acknowledgments

FROM THE BOTTOM OF MY HEART, I am so thankful to those who gave their time, energy and support into making this book a reality:

Rebecca Kaplan, my amazing editor at Abrams, for her patience, guidance, and trust.

Sarah Gifford, who designed this book, for instantly "getting" me, *Habitat*, and *Down to Earth*. You are masterful.

Berta Treitl, my agent, who has believed in me from the beginning and has gently pushed me to achieve every step of the way.

Helen Norman, my photographer, for not only beautifully capturing the homes in this book, but for being a constant friend to us and for shaping the way we view 'home.' To Matthew Dandy for assisting so kindly.

The builders, architects, craftspeople, logistics teams, and furniture manufacturers we work with have all played integral parts in turning these homes into reality. Thank you so much. Special thanks to Mike Carr of CarrMichael construction for joining us on our HGTV *Best House on the Block* journey!

Melissa Colgan, Lauren Reynolds, and Meghan Short for caring so much and tirelessly working to bring these homes to life. Some of Melissa's beautifully snapped install shots are seen in the book and I'm so thankful for her artful eye.

Our truly awesome clients, who have trusted us with their homes. And to those clients who have so generously shared their homes in this book, I can't thank you enough.

Our *Pure Style Home* readers and Instagram followers, who have come along on this journey with us and helped me find my voice. I am forever grateful.

Our friends and family, who still love us even though we don't get to see you nearly enough, and who are always there when we come up for air.

To our kids—Christian, Justin, Luke, Gisele, and Aurora—you light up every day for me and I love you like crazy.

To David, your calm, quiet strength and completely inappropriate sense of humor are what get me through everything. There's no crying in baseball and I love you.

index

Editor: Rebecca Kaplan
Designer: Sarah Gifford
Production Manager: Denise LaCongo

Library of Congress Control Number: 2018958259

ISBN: 978-1-4197-3819-7
eISBN: 978-1-68335-648-6

Printed and bound in the United States
10 9 8 7 6 5 4 3

Abrams books are available at special discounts when
purchased in quantity for premiums and promotions as
well as fundraising or educational use. Special editions
can also be created to specification. For details, contact
specialsales@abramsbooks.com or the address below.

Abrams® is a registered trademark of Harry N. Abrams, Inc.

ABRAMS
The Art of Books

195 Broadway
New York, NY 10007
abramsbooks.com